'80s & '90s ROCK

**MELODY LINE, CHORDS AND LYRICS
FOR KEYBOARD • GUITAR • VOCAL**

HAL•LEONARD•

ISBN 0-7935-9824-9

HAL•LEONARD® CORPORATION

7777 W. BLUEMOUND RD. P.O. BOX 13819 MILWAUKEE, WI 53213

Visit Hal Leonard Online at
www.halleonard.com

Welcome to the PAPERBACK SONGS SERIES.

Do you play piano, guitar, electronic keyboard, sing or play any instrument for that matter? If so, this handy "pocket tune" book is for you.

The concise, one-line music notation consists of:

MELODY, LYRICS & CHORD SYMBOLS

Whether strumming the chords on guitar, "faking" an arrangement on piano/keyboard or singing the lyrics, these fake book style arrangements can be enjoyed at any experience level – hobbyist to professional.

The musical skills necessary to successfully use this book are minimal. If you play guitar and need some help with chords, a basic chord chart is included at the back of the book.

While playing and singing is the first thing that comes to mind when using this book, it can also serve as a compact, comprehensive reference guide.

However you choose to use this PAPERBACK SONGS SERIES book, by all means have fun!

CONTENTS

(contents continued)

ALONE

Words and Music by
BILLY STEINBERG and TOM KELLY

8

al-ways got by __ on my own. __ I nev-er real-ly

cared un – til I met you, and now it

chills me to the bone. How do I get __ you a – lone?__

__ How do I get __ you a – lone? __

How do I get __ you a – lone? __

How do I get __ you a – lone, ___ a – lone, ___

__ a - lone? ___

(Instrumental)

ALWAYS

Words and Music by
JON BON JOVI

Slow Rock Ballad

This Ro - me - o is bleed - ing,
pic-tures that you left be - hind are just

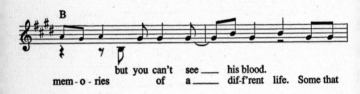

but you can't see ___ his blood.
mem - o - ries of a ___ dif-f'rent life. Some that

It's noth-ing but some feel - ings that this old ___
made us laugh, some that made us cry, one that

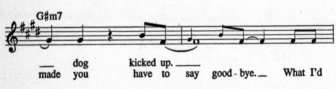

___ dog kicked up. ___
made you have to say good - bye. ___ What I'd

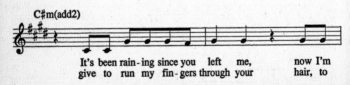

It's been rain - ing since you left me, now I'm
give to run my fin - gers through your hair, to

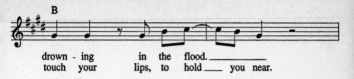

B

drown - ing   in the flood._____

touch your   lips, to hold___ you near.

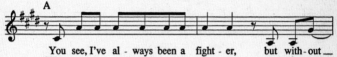

A

You see, I've al - ways been a fight - er, but with - out_

When you say your prayers, try to un - der - stand I've made_

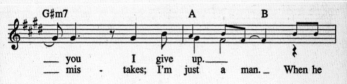

G♯m7   **A**   **B**

___ you   I give up.___

___ mis - takes; I'm just a man._ When he

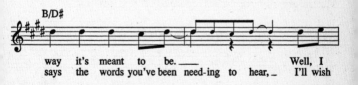

C♯m(add2)

Now I can't sing a love song   like the

holds you close, when he pulls you near,   when he

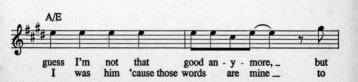

B/D♯

way it's meant to be. ___   Well, I

says the words you've been need - ing to hear, _ I'll wish

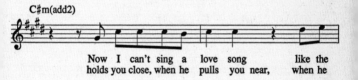

A/E

guess I'm not that good an - y - more, _ but

I was him 'cause those words are mine _ to

for you,   I could.   If you

told me to die ___ for you,   I would.

___ Take a look at my face.   There's no

price I___ won't pay   to

say these words ___ to you. _____

Guitar solo - ad lib.

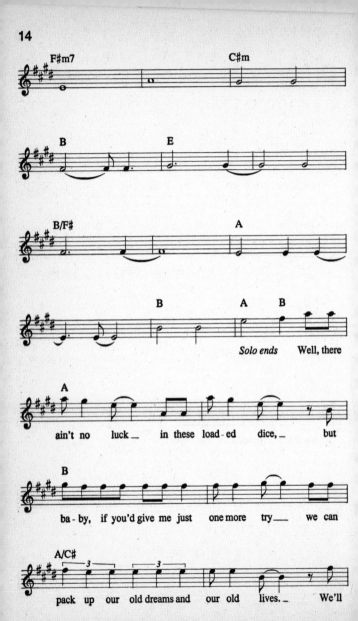

Solo ends Well, there ain't no luck __ in these load-ed dice, __ but ba-by, if you'd give me just one more try __ we can pack up our old dreams and our old lives. __ We'll

D.S. al Coda CODA

find a place where the sun still shines, yeah._ ways.

I'll be there _ 'til the stars don't shine, 'til the

heav-ens burst and the words don't rhyme. I know

when I die _ you'll be on my mind _ and I'll love you,

al - ways.
Guitar solo - ad lib.

Repeat ad lib. and Fade

Lead vocal ad lib.

ANOTHER ONE
BITES THE DUST

Words and Music by
JOHN DEACON

Steady Rock

(Instrumental)

(Sung 8va - 2nd and 3rd x)

Steve   walks wa - ri - ly down   the street with the
How do you think I'm going to get   a - long with -
(D.S.) There are plen - ty of ways you can hurt __ a man, and

brim   pulled   way down   low. __
out   you,   when you're   gone? __
bring   him   to the   ground. __

You
       You can

Ain't   no   sound   but the sound of   his   feet; __   ma -
took me for   ev - 'ry - thing that I   had __   and
beat him you can cheat him you can treat   him   bad __   and

chine   guns   rea - dy   to   go. __
kicked   me   out   on   my   own. __
leave   him   when   he's   down. __

Are you
Are you
But I'm

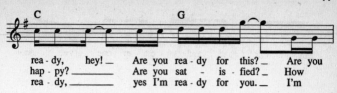

rea - dy,   hey! _   Are you rea - dy for this? _   Are you
hap - py? _____   Are you sat - is - fied? _   How
rea - dy, _____   yes I'm rea - dy for you. _   I'm

hang - ing on the edge of your seat? _
long   can you stand   the heat? _
stand - ing on my own   two feet. _

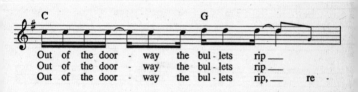

Out of the door - way   the bul - lets rip _
Out of the door - way   the bul - lets rip _
Out of the door - way   the bul - lets rip, _   re -

to the sound of the beat. _
to the sound of the beat. _   An -
peat - ing the sound of the beat. _

oth - er one bites the dust. _   An -

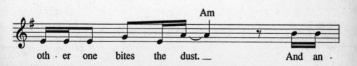

oth - er one bites the dust. _   And an -

18

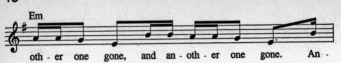

oth - er one gone, and an - oth - er one gone. An -

oth - er one bites the dust. ___

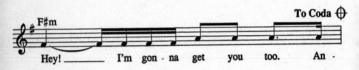

Hey! ___ I'm gon - na get you too. An -

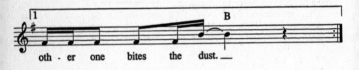

oth - er one bites the dust. ___

oth - er one bites the dust. ___

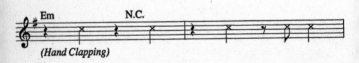

(Hand Clapping)

An -

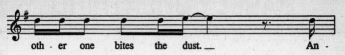

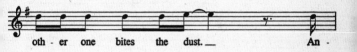

D.S. al Coda

CODA

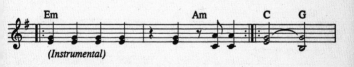

(Instrumental)

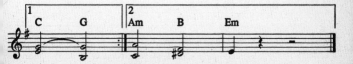

BARELY BREATHING

Words and Music by
DUNCAN SHEIK

Well, I know what you're do - ing. I see it all _ too clear.
- sion, so com-plete-ly torn. _
- ing what's it all _ a - bout. _

I on - ly taste _ the sa -
It must have been _ that yes -
It used to be _ so cer -

- line when I kiss a - way _ your tears.
- ter-day was the day that I _ was born.
- tain. Now I can't fig - ure out,

You real - ly had _ me go -
There's not _ much to _ ex - am -
what _ is this _ at - trac -

ing, wish-ing on a star. _ The black holes that _ sur-round
ine, noth-ing left to hide. _ You real - ly can't be se -
tion? Don't it fill the day, _ and noth - ing left to rea -

Fmaj9

care. And I ___ could stand ___ here wait-

C(add2)

ing, ooh, ___ for an - oth - er day.

G(add2)

I don't ___ sup - pose ___ it's worth.

Am7

___ the price, ___ it's worth ___ the price, ___ the price ___

Fmaj9

___ that I ___ would pay. ___

1.

D.S.

And ev - 'ry - one ___ keeps ask -

24

is it friend or foe? ___ I rise a - bove,

I sink be - low, ___ and ev - 'ry time

you come and go. ___ Please don't

come and go. ___

'Cause I ___ am bare - ly breath -

D.S.S. al Coda

CODA

And I know what you're do - ing.

I see it all ___ too clear.

BUILDING A MYSTERY

Words and Music by SARAH McLACHLAN
and PIERRE MARCHAND

D   **A**

___ shad - ow get - ting in ___ the way? ___
___ eve - ning stayed.

Esus   **E**   **G(add2)**

You're_ so beau-ti- ful, __ with an edge and charm - ing.
You're_ a beau-ti- ful, __ a beau-ti - ful fucked-up man.

Esus   **E**   **G(add2)**   **A**

You're so care - ful when I'm in your arms ___
You set it up, you're ra - zor wire_ sharp ___

Bm   **G**   **D**   **A**

___ } 'cause you're work-ing build-ing __ a mys - ter - y,___

Bm   **G**   **D**   **A**

___ hold - ing on ___ and hold - ing it __ in.

Bm   **G**   **D**   **A**

___ Yeah, you're work-ing build-ing__ a mys - ter - y ___

1

Bm   **G**   **D**   **A**

___ and choos - ing so ___ care - ful - ly. ___

care - ful - ly   Yeah, you're work-ing

build-ing __ a mys - ter - y, _____ hold - ing on __

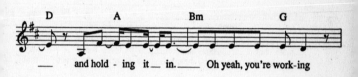

__ and hold - ing it __ in. __ Oh yeah, you're work-ing

build - ing ____ a mys - ter - y _____

__ and choos - ing   so __ care - ful - ly. __

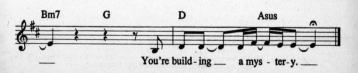

__ You're build - ing __ a mys - ter-y. __

CANDLE IN THE WIND 1997

Music by ELTON JOHN
Words by BERNIE TAUPIN

In a slow 2

Good-bye, Eng-land's rose; ____ may you ev - er
Love - li - ness we've lost; ____ these emp - ty days
Good-bye, Eng-land's rose; ____ may you ev - er

grow in our hearts. __ You were the grace that
with - out __ your smile. __ This torch we'll al - ways
grow in our hearts. __ You were the grace that

placed it - self __ where lives were torn a - part. __
car - ry for our na - tion's gold - en child..
placed it - self __ where lives were torn a - part. __

You called out to our
And e - ven though we

coun - try, and you whis-pered
try, the
Good - bye, Eng - land's rose, __ from a coun - try lost

32

CHANGE THE WORLD

featured on the Motion Picture Soundtrack PHENOMENON

Words and Music by GORDON KENNEDY,
TOMMY SIMS and WAYNE KIRKPATRICK

CRIMINAL

Words and Music by
FIONA APPLE

Moderately

I've been a bad, __ bad __ girl;
Heav-en help __ me for the way I am;

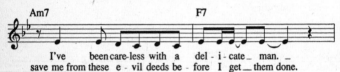

I've been care-less with a del-i-cate man. __
save me from these e-vil deeds be-fore I get __ them done.

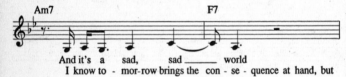

And it's a sad, sad __ world
I know to-mor-row brings the con-se-quence at hand, but

when a girl will break a boy __ just be-cause she can. __
I keep liv-in' this day like the next will nev-er come. __ Oh,

Don't you tell me to __ de-ny __ it; I've done wrong, __
help me, but don't tell me to __ de-ny __ it; I've got-ta cleanse __

__ and I wan-na suf-fer for __ my __ sins.
__ my-self of all __ these lies till I'm good e-nough for him.

37

Cm7

(Instrumental)

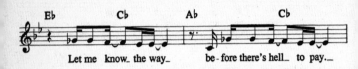

Eb   **Cb**   **Ab**   **Cb**

Let me know_ the way_   be - fore there's hell_ to pay._

Eb   **Cb**   **Ab7**

Give me room_ to lay_ the law_ and let _ me go. _

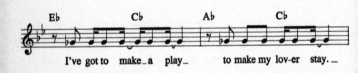

Eb   **Cb**   **Ab**   **Cb**

I've got to make_a play_   to make my lov-er stay. _

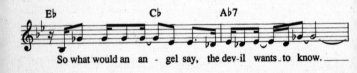

Eb   **Cb**   **Ab7**

So what would an an - gel say, the dev-il wants_to know. _____

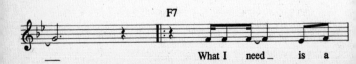

F7

_   What I   need _   is   a

DON'T LOOK BACK IN ANGER

Words and Music by
NOEL GALLAGHER

Slip in- side ___ the eye of your mind, ___
Take me to ___ the place where you go, ___

don't you know you might ___ find ___
where no- bod- y knows ___

a bet-ter place to play. ___
if it's night or day. ___

You said ___ that you'd ___ nev- er been, ___
Please don't put your life in the hands ___

but all the things that you've seen ___
of a rock 'n' roll band ___

slow-ly fade a- way. ___
who'll throw it all a- way. ___

(1.) So I
(2.) I'm gon- na } start a rev- o- lu- tion from my

(D.S.) *Instrumental solo*

42

EVERY BREATH YOU TAKE

Written and Composed by
STING

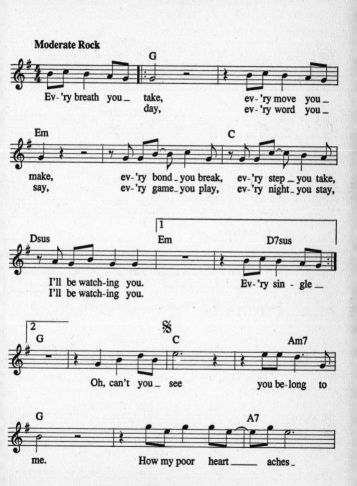

with ev-'ry step _ you take. Ev-'ry move you _

make, ev-'ry vow you _ break,

ev-'ry smile _ you fake, ev-'ry claim _ you stake,

I'll be watch-ing you.

Since you've gone, _ I been lost _ with-out _____ a trace.

I dream at night I can on - ly see _ your face.

I look a-round but it's you I can't _ re-place,

I feel so cold and I long for your _ em-brace.

DON'T SPEAK

**Words and Music by ERIC STEFANI
and GWEN STEFANI**

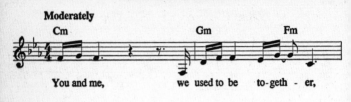

You and me, we used to be to-geth-er,

ev-'ry day to-geth-er, al-ways. I

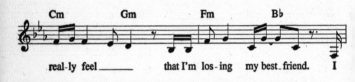

real-ly feel _____ that I'm los-ing my best friend. I

can't be-lieve this could be the _____ end. It

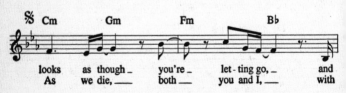

looks as though _____ you're let-ting go, _____ and
As we die, _____ both _____ you and I, _____ with

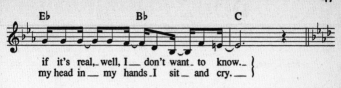

if it's real,_ well, I_ don't want_ to know._
my head in_ my hands_I sit_ and cry._

Don't speak, I know_ just what_ you're say -

- ing, so_ please stop_ ex - plain -

- ing. Don't tell me 'cause_ it hurts._

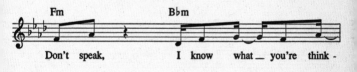

Don't speak, I know what_ you're think -

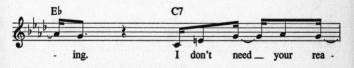

- ing. I don't need_ your rea -

To Coda ⊕

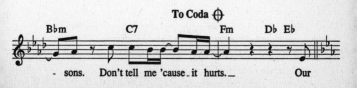

- sons. Don't tell me 'cause_ it hurts._ Our

48

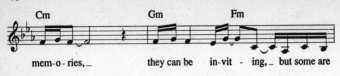

Cm   Gm   Fm

mem-o-ries, __   they can be in-vit - ing, __ but some are

D.S. al Coda

Bb   Gm   Fm   Bb

al - to-geth - er might - y   fright - 'ning.

CODA

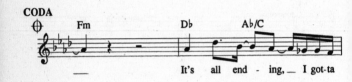

Fm   Db   Ab/C

__   It's   all end - ing, __ I got-ta

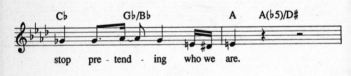

Cb   Gb/Bb   A   A(b5)/D#

stop   pre-tend - ing   who we are.

Play 3 times

Ab   Cm Gm   Fm   Bb

Instrumental solo

Gm Cm   Fm   Cm   Gm

Solo ends You and me,

Fm   Bb   Fm   Bb

I can see us dy - ing... are __ we? __

FAST CAR

Words and Music by
TRACY CHAPMAN

Moderately

Dmaj7   A5

You got a fast _____ car.
You got a fast _____ car.
my old man's _ got a prob - lem.   He

F#m   E(add4)

I want a tick - et to an - y - where.
I got a plan to get us out of here.   Been
live with the bot - tle, that's the way it is.   He says his

Dmaj7   A5

May - be we make a deal. _____
work - ing at the con - ven - ience store.
bod - y's too old for work - ing;   his

F#m   E(add4)

May - be to - geth - er we can get some - where. _
Man - aged to save _____ just a lit - tle bit of mon - ey.
bod - y's too young _____ to look like his.   My

Dmaj7   A5

An - y - place is bet - ter; _____
Won't have to drive too far,   just
ma - ma went off and left him.   She

51

F#m   E(add4)

leave   to - night __ or live and die   this   way.

%

Dmaj7   A5   F#m   E(add4)

(Instrumental)

Dmaj7   A5

I re-mem-ber when we were

D

driv - ing,   driv - ing in your   car, __

A

speed   so   fast __ I   felt like __ I   was drunk.

F#m

cit - y lights lay   out   be - fore __ us and your

Esus   D   F#m

arms felt nice wrapped 'round my shoul-der. And I _____ had a

E   D   F#m

feel-ing that I __ be-longed. __ I _____ had a

Dmaj7　　　　　A5

We'll move out＿ of the shel - ter.
got no plans,＿ I ain't go - ing no - where so

1. F#m　　　　　E(add4)

buy a big house and live in the sub - urbs.

2. F#m　　　　　E(add4)　　　　　**D.S. al Coda**

take your fast car and keep on driv - ing.＿

CODA

Dmaj7　　　　　A5

You got a fast＿ car. Is it

F#m　　　　　E(add4)

fast e - nough＿ so you could fly a - way?＿

Dmaj7　　　　　A5

You got - ta make a de - ci - sion;

F#m　　　　　E(add4)

leave to - night＿ or live and die this way.

Play 3 times

Dmaj7　A5　　F#m E(add4)　　Dmaj7　　A

(Instrumental)

GALILEO

Words and Music by
EMILY SALIERS

56

ar - an - ni - hi - la - tion in my

life - time. I'm still _ not right. _ *(Instrumental)*

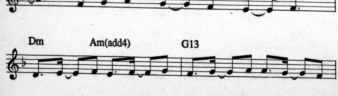

vi - sion, king of in - sight? _____

How __ long? _____ How __

long? _____ How __

long? _____

FIELDS OF GOLD

Written and Composed by
STING

walk   in   fields __   of gold.   *(Instrumental)*

Man - y   years have   passed   since those __
mem - ber   me   when the __

__ sum - mer days   a - mong   the   fields __   of bar -
__ west wind moves   up - on   the   fields __   of bar -

GIRLFRIEND

Words and Music by
MATTHEW SWEET

66

You're on-ly look-in' for some-one to love._

_ 'Cause you need _ to be

back in the arms _ of a good _ friend.

(Instrumental)

And I'm _ nev - er gon-na set you free._

_ No,_ I'm nev - er gon-na set you free. _

HAND IN MY POCKET

Lyrics by ALANIS MORISSETTE
Music by ALANIS MORISSETTE and GLEN BALLARD

Moderate Rock

I'm broke but I'm__ hap - py, ___ I'm
drunk but I'm__ so - ber, ___ I'm

Instrumental solo
free but I'm__ fo - cused,. I'm

poor but I'm kind, ___ I'm
young and I'm un - der - paid, I'm

green but I'm wise, ___ I'm

short but I'm_ health - y, yeah. ___ I'm
tired but I'm_ work - ing, yeah. ___ I

hard but I'm_ friend - ly, ba - by. I'm

high but I'm ground - ed, I'm
care but I'm rest - less, I'm

sad but I'm laugh - ing, I'm

sane but I'm o - ver - whelmed, I'm
here but I'm real - ly ___ gone, I'm

brave but I'm chick - en ___ shit, I'm

lost but I'm hope - ful, ba -
wrong and I'm sor - ry, ba -
sick but I'm pret - ty, ba -

- by. What it all comes down __ to
- by. What it all comes down __ to
Solo ends What it all comes down __ to
- by. What it all boils down __ to

is that ev - 'ry-thing's gon - na be
is that ev - 'ry-thing's gon - na be
is that I have - n't got it all fig - ured
is that no one's real - ly got it fig - ured

fine, fine, fine. _____ I've got
quite al - right. _____ I've got
out just yet. _____ I've got
out just yet. _____ I've got

one hand in my pock - et and the
one hand in my pock - et and the
one hand in my pock - et and the
one hand in my pock - et and the

oth - er one is giv - ing a high five.
oth - er one is flick - ing a cig - a - rette.
oth - er one is giv - ing the peace sign.
oth - er one is play - ing the pi - a - no.

GIVE ME ONE REASON

Words and Music by
TRACY CHAPMAN

I called too man-y times. _____
They might take a - way _ my life. _____
oh, and give you what _ you _ need. _
Oh, give me just one rea-son _ why _ I _ should stay.

To Coda

You can call me, ba - by. You can
I just want some-one to hold me,
But I'm too old to go chas-ing you a -
Said I told you that I loved you, _

call me an - y - time. _____ But you got to
oh, and rock me through the
round, wast - ing my pre - cious en - er -

call _____ me.
night. _____
gy. _____

(1.,3.) Give me one rea - son to stay here _____
(2.) Instrumental solo

and I'll turn right back a - round. _

(You could see me turn-ing.) Give me one rea-son to stay here _____

73

HIT ME WITH YOUR BEST SHOT

Words and Music by
EDDIE SCHWARTZ

HOLD MY HAND

Words and Music by DARIUS CARLOS RUCKER,
EVERETT DEAN FELBER, MARK WILLIAM BRYAN
and JAMES GEORGE SONEFELD

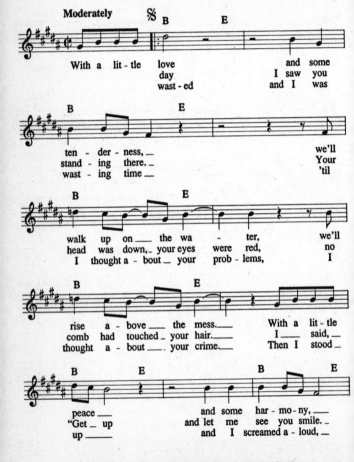

(Hold ___ my hand.) ___ { I'll take you
{ I'll take you

(Hold ___ my hand.) ___

to a place ___ where you ___ can be ___
to the prom - ised land. ___

an - y-thing you wan - na be ___ be-cause
May-be we can't change ___ the world, but {

I wan - na love you ___ the best that, the

To Coda ⊕

best that I can. ___

(Instrumental)

D.S. al Coda

See, I was

HOW AM I SUPPOSED TO LIVE WITHOUT YOU

Words and Music by MICHAEL BOLTON
and DOUG JAMES

Slowly

I could hard - ly be - lieve ___ it when I
I'm too proud for cry - ing, did - n't

heard the news ___ to - day. I
come here to break down. It's just a

had to come and get it straight from you. ___
dream of mine is com-in' to ___ an end. ___

They said you are leav - in', some-one's
And how can I blame ___ you when I

swept your heart ___ a - way. ___ From the
built my world a - round ___ the hope that one

I DON'T WANT TO WAIT

Words and Music by
PAULA COLE

So o- pen up your morn- ing light and say a lit- tle prayer for I. You know that if we are to stay a- live, then see the peace in ev- 'ry eye.

Du du du du du, du du du du du, du du du du du du.

She had two_ ba-bies, one was six_ months, one_was three,
He showed up _ all wet on the rain - y front_ step

in the war___ of for-ty - four. ___
wear-ing shrap - nel in his skin. ___

Ev-'ry tel - e-phone ring,
And the war_ he saw

ev - 'ry heart - beat sting - ing when she
lives_ in-side_ him still. _ It's so

thought_ it was God_ call-ing her. ___ Oh, would_
hard ___ to be gen - tle and warm. _ The years_

_ her son ___ grow_ to know his fa -
_ pass by, ___ and now_ he has ___ grand -

ther?
daugh - ters. _____

I don't want to wait for our lives

to be o - ver. I want

to know right now, what will it be?

I don't want to wait for our lives

to be o - ver. Will it

be yes, or will it be....

sor - ry? Du du du du du,

92

I STILL HAVEN'T FOUND
WHAT I'M LOOKING FOR

Words by BONO
Music by U2

Moderately, with a steady beat

scaled _ these cit-y walls, _ these cit-y
held the hand of the dev – il. It was warm in
cross of my shame, of my

Gsus2　　　　　　　　　　　　　　**D5**

walls, _____ on – ly to be with _ you. _
the night; _ I was cold as a stone. _
shame. _ You know I be – lieve it.

Asus　　　　　　**Gsus2**

But I still _____ have–n't found _ what I'm look-

D　　**Dsus**　**D**　　　　　**Asus**

ing for. _____ But I still _____ have–n't found _

1

To Coda ⊕

D/G　**Gsus2**　　　　**D**　　**Dsus**　**D**

_ what I'm look-ing for. _____ I have

2 **D5**　　　　　　　　**G**　**D**　　　　**G**　**D**

_ *(Instrumental)*

　　　　　G　**D**　　　　**G**　**D**　　　　**G**　**D**

D.S. al Coda

I be -

CODA

But I still _____ have-n't found__

_____ what I'm look - ing for. _____

But I still _____ have-n't found__

_____ what I'm look - ing for. _____

Repeat and Fade

(Instrumental)

I WANT TO KNOW WHAT LOVE IS

Words and Music by
MICK JONES

Moderately

I've got-ta take a lit-tle time, _ a lit-tle

time to think _ things o - ver.

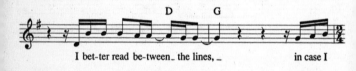

I bet-ter read be-tween _ the lines, _ in case I

need it when _ I'm old - er. _

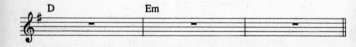

trav-eled so far __ to change this lone - ly life. __

I want to know what love __ is. __

I want you to show __

__ me. I want to feel what love __ is. __

I know you can show __

__ me. __

D.S. and Fade

__ me.

KING OF PAIN

Written and Composed by
STING

Moderately fast

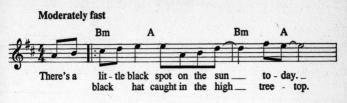

There's a lit - tle black spot on the sun ___ to - day. _
black hat caught in the high ___ tree - top.

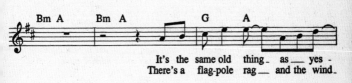

It's the same old thing _ as ___ yes -
There's a flag-pole rag _ and the wind

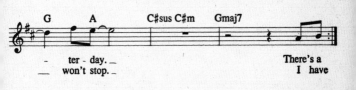

_ ter - day. ___ There's a
_ won't stop. _ I have

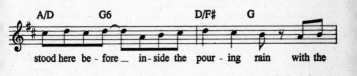

stood here be - fore in - side the pour - ing rain with the

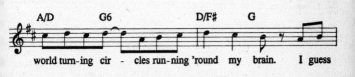

world turn-ing cir - cles run - ning 'round my brain. I guess

king of pain. ___ There's a king ___ on a throne ___

___ with his eyes ___ torn out, ___ there's a blind ___ man look-

- ing for a shad-ow of doubt, there's a rich ___ man sleep-

- ing on a gold-en bed, there's a skel-e-ton chok-

- ing on a crust of ___ bread.

(Instrumental)

D.S. al Coda

There's a

CODA

lit-tle black spot on the sun.___

to - day. It's the same old thing as yes - ter - day.

I have stood here be - fore inside the pour - ing rain with the world turn-ing cir - cles run-ning 'round my brain. I guess I'm al-ways hop - ing that you'll end this reign, but it's my des - ti - ny to be the king of pain.

Repeat and Fade

King of pain.

IF I EVER LOSE
MY FAITH IN YOU

Written and Composed by
STING

Moderately

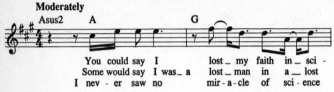

You could say I lost _ my faith in _ sci-
Some would say I was a lost _ man in a _ lost
I nev-er saw no mir-a-cle of sci-ence

ence and prog-ress.
world.

You could say I lost my be-lief in the ho-ly _ church.
You could say I lost my _ faith in the peo-ple on T.V.
that did-n't go from a bless-ing to a curse.

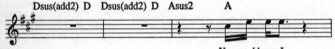

You could say I
You could say I lost my be-
I nev-er saw no

To Coda

lost _ my sense of di-rec-tion.
-lief _ in our pol-i-ti-cians.
mil-i-tar-y so-lu-tion

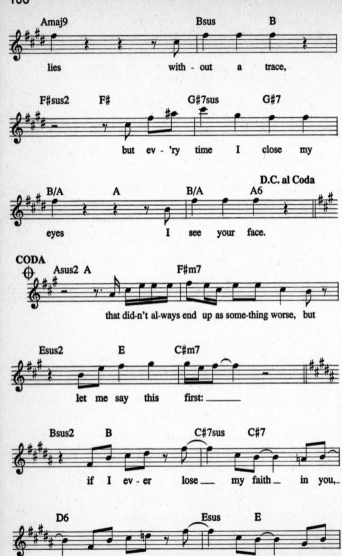

there'd be noth-ing left ___ for me ___ to do,

there'd be noth-ing left ___ for me ___ to do.

If I ev - er lose ___ my faith, ___

if I ev - er lose ___ my faith, ___

if I ev - er lose ___ my faith, ___

if I ev - er lose ___ my faith ___

Repeat and Fade

in you...

IRONIC

Lyrics by ALANIS MORISSETTE
Music by ALANIS MORISSETTE and GLEN BALLARD

An old man turned nine-ty - eight.__ He won the
Play It Safe was a-fraid to fly.__ He packed his
traf - fic jam when you're al - read-y late.__ A no

lot - ter - y, and died the next__ day. It's a
suit - case and kissed his kids good - bye. He wait-ed
smok-ing sign on your cig - a - rette break. It's like

black fly __ in your Char-don-nay. It's a
his whole damn life to take that flight, __ and as the
ten thou - sand spoons when all you need is a knife. It's

death row __ par - don __ two
plane crashed __ down, he thought, "Well,
meet-ing the man of my dreams, and then

min - utes too __ late. } Is - n't it i -
is - n't this __ nice..." }

Fmaj7

life has a fun - ny way___ of help-ing you out___

G6

___ when you think___ ev - 'ry - thing's___ gone wrong___ and

Fmaj7   **C**   **D.S. al Coda**

ev - 'ry-thing blows___ up in___ your face._____

A

CODA

G/B   **Am7**

meet-ing his beau - ti - ful wife.

G/B   **C(add2)**

And is - n't it i - ron-ic... don't you

G/B   **Am7**   **G/B**   **C(add2)**

think? A lit-tle too i - ron-ic. And yeah, I

G/B   **Am7**   **G**   **C**

real-ly do think it's like rain_____ on your

G   **Am7**   **G**   **C**

wed-ding___ day. It's a free___ ride_____ when you're

LET HER CRY

**Words and Music by DARIUS CARLOS RUCKER,
EVERETT DEAN FELBER, MARK WILLIAM BRYAN
and JAMES GEORGE SONEFELD**

Moderately slow Rock

She sits a-lone by a lamp - post ___
try'n to find a thought that's es - caped ___ her mind. ___
She says, "Dad's ___ the one I ___ love ___
___ the most, ___
but Stipe's ___ not far be - hind." ___

She nev - er lets me in, ___
This morn - ing I woke up a - lone, ___
Last night I tried to leave, ___

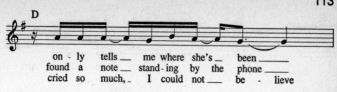

D

on - ly tells __ me where she's __ been _____
found a note __ stand - ing by the phone ____
cried so much, _ I could not __ be - lieve

C(add2)   **G**

when she's had _ too much to drink.____
say - in', "May-be, may-be I'll be back some-day."
she was the same girl I fell in love with long a - go.

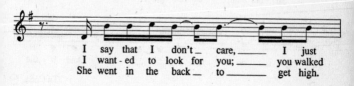

I say that I don't __ care, _____ I just
I want - ed to look for you; _____ you walked
She went in the back __ to _____ get high.

D

run my hands through her dark hair, __ and I
in. I did - n't know just what to do, __ so I
I sat down on my couch and cried, _ yell - ing,

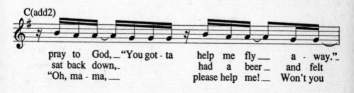

C(add2)

pray to God, _ "You got - ta help me fly __ a - way."
sat back down, _ had a beer _ and felt
"Oh, ma - ma, __ please help me! Won't you

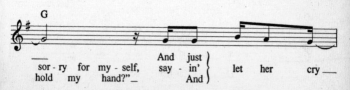

G

__ And just
sor - ry for my - self, say - in' { let her cry __
hold my hand?" _ And }

LOVE IS A BATTLEFIELD

Words and Music by
MIKE CHAPMAN and HOLLY KNIGHT

Moderate Rock

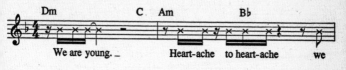

We are young. ___ Heart-ache to heart-ache we

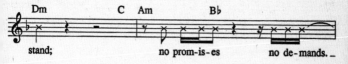

stand; no prom-is-es no de-mands. ___

___ Love is a bat-tle-field.

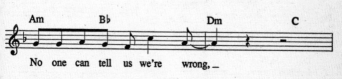

We are ___ strong.

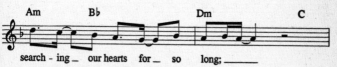

No one can tell us we're wrong, ___

search - ing ___ our hearts for ___ so long; _____

LINGER

Lyrics by DOLORES O'RIORDAN
Music by DOLORES O'RIORDAN and NOEL HOGAN

Moderately (not too fast)

If you, ____ if you could re-turn, don't let it burn, ____ don't let it fade.. I'm sure I'm not be-ing rude, ____ but it's just your at-ti-tude.. It's tear-ing me ____ a-part, ____ it's ru-in-ing ev-'ry-thing. I swore, ____ I swore I would be true, if you could get by ____

and hon-ey, so did you. _____ So
try-ing not to lie, _____

why _____ were you hold - ing _____ her
things _____ would - n't be so _____ con -

hand? _____ Is that the way _____ we stand? _____
fused _____ and I would - n't feel _____ so used,

_____ Were you ly - ing all _____ the time?
_____ but you al - ways real - ly knew

_____ Was it just a game _____ to you?
_____ I just wan - na be _____ with you.

_____ But I'm in _____ so deep.

You know I'm such a fool _____ for you.

120

LIVIN' ON A PRAYER

Words and Music by JON BON JOVI,
RICHIE SAMBORA and DESMOND CHILD

Moderate Rock

124

LOVE SNEAKIN' UP ON YOU

Words and Music by JIMMY SCOTT
and TOM SNOW

Rain - y night,__ I'm all a - lone,__
No - where on earth __ for your heart to hide

sit - ting here wait - ing for your voice on the__ phone.__
once love comes sneak - in' up on your blind __ side, __

Fe - ver turns __ to cold,__ cold sweat,__
and you might as well __ try to stop__ the rain__ or

think - ing a - bout __ the things we ain't done yet. __
stand in the tracks __ of a __ run - a - way train. __

Tell me now,__ I've got to know. Do you feel the same?__
You just can't fight __ it when a thing is meant to be. __

(D.S.) *Guitar solo*

Do you just light up at the men - tion of my name?_
So come on, let's fin - ish what you start - ed with me.__
Solo ends

Don't wor - ry, ba - by. It ain't noth - ing new. _

That's just love _ sneak - in' up on you. __ If your

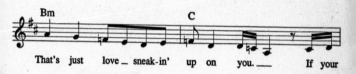

whole world _ is shak - in' _ and you feel like _ I do, ___

that's just love __ sneak - in' up on you. __ Hey, hey. __

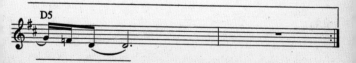

128

REAL LOVE

Words and Music by
JOHN LENNON

Moderately slow

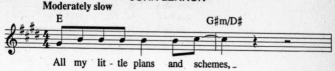

All my lit-tle plans and schemes, _ lost like some for-got-ten dreams.

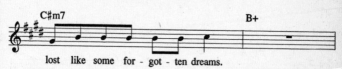

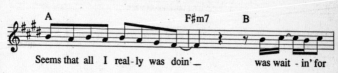

Seems that all I real-ly was doin' _ was wait-in' for you. _

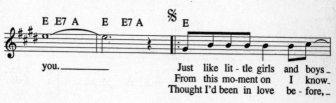

Just like lit-tle girls and boys _
From this mo-ment on I know _
Thought I'd been in love be-fore, _

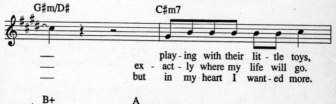

play-ing with their lit-tle toys,
ex-act-ly where my life will go.
but in my heart I want-ed more.

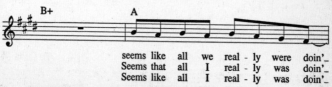

seems like all we real-ly were doin' _
Seems that all I real-ly was doin' _
Seems like all I real-ly was doin' _

130

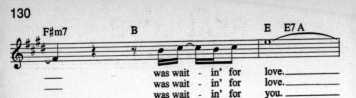

was wait - in' for love.____
was wait - in' for love.____
was wait - in' for you. ____

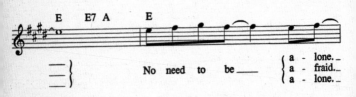

No need to be ____ { a - lone.
{ a - fraid.
{ a - lone.

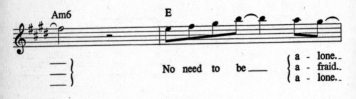

No need to be ____ { a - lone.
{ a - fraid.
{ a - lone.

It's real ____ love.

It's real.____ Yes, it's real ____ love.

1 A · B · Em

— It's real. _____ *(Instrumental)*

B · Em · B

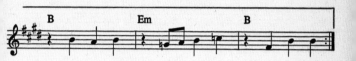

2 A · B · F#m7

— It's real. _____ *Instrumental solo*

C# · F#m · Bsus

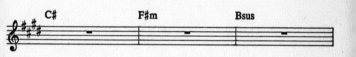

D.S. al Coda
B

CODA
A · B

Solo ends · — It's real. _____

Repeat and Fade

E · C#m · A · B

— Yes, it's real ____ love. — It's real. _____

LOVEFOOL

Music by PETER SVENSSON
Lyrics by NINA PERSSON and PETER SVENSSON

Moderate Rock

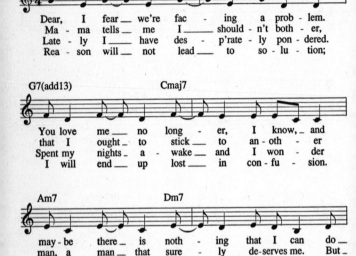

Dear, I fear we're fac — ing a prob — lem.
Ma — ma tells me I should — n't both — er,
Late — ly I have des — p'rate — ly pon — dered,
Rea — son will not lead to so — lu — tion;

You love me no long — er, I know, and
that I ought to stick to an — oth — er
Spent my nights a — wake and I won — der
I will end up lost in con — fu — sion.

may — be there is noth — ing that I can do.
man, a man that sure — ly de — serves me. But
what I could have done in an — oth — er way.
I don't care if you real — ly care as long

— to make you do.
— I think you do.
— to make you stay.
— as you don't go.

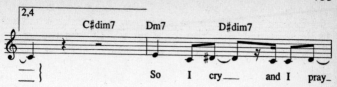

So I cry __ and I pray __

__ and I beg. __ (Love me, love __ me,) say __

__ that you love me. (Fool me, fool __ me,) go __

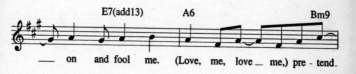

__ on and fool me. (Love, me, love __ me,) pre - tend __

__ that you love me. (Leave me, leave __ me,) just say __

__ that you need me. __ So I cry __

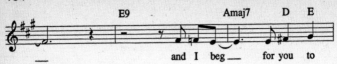

and I beg ___ for you to

(love me, love ___ me.) Say ___ that you love me.

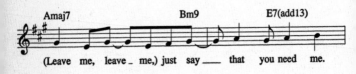

(Leave me, leave ___ me,) just say ___ that you need me.

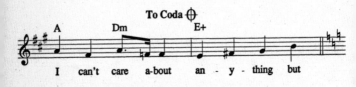

To Coda ⊕

I can't care a-bout an - y - thing but

D.C. al Coda

you. _____

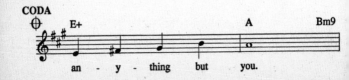

CODA ⊕

an - y - thing but you.

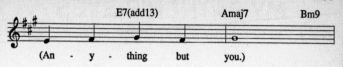

(An - y - thing but you.)

(Love me, love __ me,) say

that you love me. __ (Fool me, fool __ me,)

go on and fool me. (Love me, love __ me,)

I know that you need me. I can't care a-bout

an - y - thing but you.

MY FATHER'S EYES

Words and Music by
ERIC CLAPTON

Moderately

B   **E**   **F#**   **B**

Sail - ing down   be - hind the sun,
Then the light   be - gins to shine
Then the jag -   ged edge ap - pears

C#/E#   **E**   **F#**   **B**

wait - ing for __ my   prince __ to come. __
and I hear those an - cient   lul - la - bies. __
through the dis - tant   clouds __ of tears. __

E   **F#**   **G#m**

Pray - ing __ for __ the heal - ing rain
And as __ I watch this seed - ling grow,
And I'm like a bridge that __ was washed a - way.

C#/E#   **D/F#**   **A/E**   **E**

to re - store __ my soul a - gain. __
feel my heart start to o - ver - flow. __
My foun - da - tions were made of clay. __

C#m   **Amaj7**   **F#m7**   **B**

Just a toe rag   on __ the __ run.
Where do I find   the words to say?
And as my soul   slides down to die,

CODA

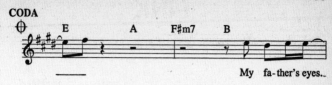

My fa-ther's eyes..

(Looked in - to __ my fa - ther's eyes.) __
My fa-ther's eyes..

I looked in - to my __ fa -

- ther's eyes.
(Looked in - to my fa - ther's eyes.) __
My fa-ther's eyes..

(Looked in - to __ my fa -

Repeat and Fade

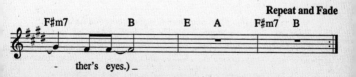

- ther's eyes.) __

PINK

Words and Music by STEVEN TYLER,
RICHIE SUPA and GLEN BALLARD

Moderately

Pink, it's my new ob-ses-sion.

Pink, it's not e-ven a ques-tion. Put

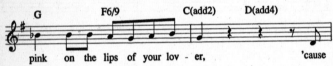

pink on the lips of your lov-er, 'cause

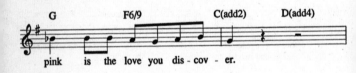

pink is the love you dis-cov-er.

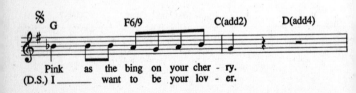

Pink as the bing on your cher-ry.
(D.S.) I _____ want to be your lov-er.

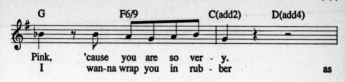

| G | F6/9 | C(add2) | D(add4) |

Pink,   'cause you are so ver - y.
I   wan-na wrap you in rub - ber   as

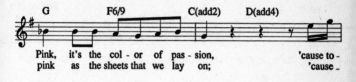

| G | F6/9 | C(add2) | D(add4) |

Pink,   it's the col - or of pas - sion,   'cause to -
pink   as the sheets that we lay on;   'cause

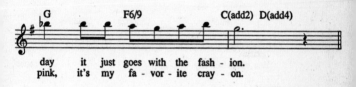

| G | F6/9 | C(add2) D(add4) |

day   it just goes with the fash - ion.
pink,   it's my fa - vor - ite cray - on.

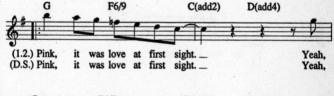

| G | F6/9 | C(add2) | D(add4) |

(1.2.) Pink,   it was love at first sight. __   Yeah,
(D.S.) Pink,   it was love at first sight. __   Yeah,

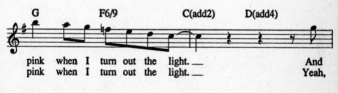

| G | F6/9 | C(add2) | D(add4) |

pink when I turn out the light. __   And
pink when I turn out the light. __   Yeah,

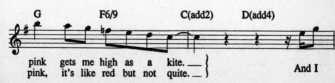

| G | F6/9 | C(add2) | D(add4) |

pink gets me high as a kite. __ }
pink, it's like red but not quite. __ }   And I

think ev - 'ry-thing is go - ing to be_ all right_

_ no mat - ter what_ we do_ to - night._

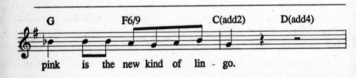

_ You could be my fla - min - go, 'cause

pink is the new kind of lin - go.

Pink, like a de - co um - brel - la; it's

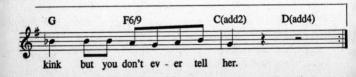

kink but you don't ev - er tell her.

(Instrumental)

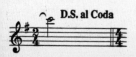

D.S. al Coda

CODA

THE RIVER OF DREAMS

Words and Music by
BILLY JOEL

Smooth Shuffle, with soul

In the mid-dle of the night ___ I go walk-ing in my
night ___ I go walk-ing in my

sleep, _____ from the moun-tains of faith ___
sleep, _____ through the val - ley of fear ___

to a riv - er so
to a riv - er so

deep. _____ I must be look-ing for some -
deep. _____ And I've been search-ing for some -

- thing, _____ some-thing sa - cred I lost.
- thing _____ tak - en out of my soul, ___

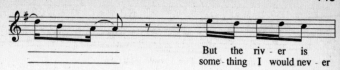

But the riv - er is
some - thing I would nev - er

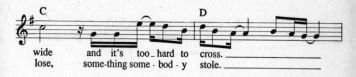

C   D

wide   and it's too hard to   cross. _____
lose,   some-thing some - bod - y   stole. _____

Em   D6

And e - ven though I know the riv - er is wide _ I walk
I don't know why I go walk-ing at night, _ but now I'm
I'm   not sure a - bout a life af - ter this, _ God knows _

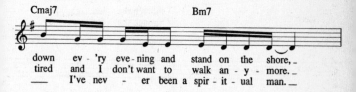

Cmaj7   Bm7

down   ev - 'ry eve - ning and   stand on the   shore, _
tired   and I don't want to   walk an - y - more. _
_____ I've nev - er been a spir - it - ual man. _

Cmaj7   Bm7

and try to cross   to the op - po - site side _ so I can
I hope it does-n't take the rest of my life _ un - til I
Bap - tized _ by the fire I ___ wade _ in - to the

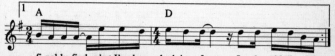

1   A   D

fi - nal-ly find _ what I've been look-ing for. _ In the mid-dle of the

that it can on-ly be
We're all ___ car-ried a -

seen ___ by the eyes of the
long ___ by the riv - er of

To Coda

blind, ___ in the mid-dle of the night. ___
dreams, ___ in the mid-dle of the

(Instrumental)

D.S. al Coda
(take 2nd ending)

CODA

G

(I go walk-ing in the, in the mid-dle of the;
night. _____

I go walk-ing in the, in the mid-dle of the;

C

I go walk-ing in the, in the mid-dle of the;

Repeat and Fade

D

I go walk-ing in the, in the mid-dle of the;)

ROLL TO ME

Words and Music by
JUSTIN CURRIE

Look a-round your world, pretty ba-by. Is it
look in-to your heart, pretty ba-by. Is it

ev-'ry-thing you hoped it-'d be?
ach-ing with some name-less need? Is there

The wrong guy, the wrong sit-u-a-tion,
some-thing wrong and you can't put your fin-ger on it?

the right time to roll to me,
Right then, roll to

roll to me. And

me. And I don't think I have

150

151

SEMI-CHARMED LIFE

Words and Music by
STEPHAN JENKINS

G   D

And I'll make you smile, like a drug for you.
stop, I won't come down. I keep stock with the
__ me cry. __

C

Do ev - er what you want to do. com-ing o - ver
tick - tock rhy-thm, a bump for the drop, and then I
When I'm with you I feel ___ like I could die, __

G   D

you. Keep on smil - ing what we go through.
bumped up. I took the hit that I was giv-en, then I
__ and that _ would be all ___ right,

C   To Coda I ⊕

One stop to the rhy-thm that di - vides you.
bumped a - gain, _ then I bumped a - gain. I said
all right. ___ And when the

1.
G   D

And I speak to you __ like the cho - rus to the

C

verse. Chop an - oth - er line like a co - da with a

G   D

curse. Come on like a freak show takes the stage.

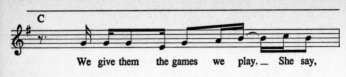

We give them the games we play.— She say,

G D C

"I want some - thing_ else to get me through this

G D C

sem-i-charmed kind of life,— ba - by, ba - by.

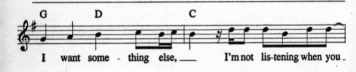

G D C

I want some - thing else,— I'm not lis-tening when you_

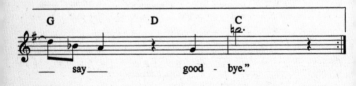

G D C

_ say_ good - bye."

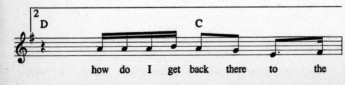

2

D C

how do I get back there to the

place where I ___ fell a-sleep in-side you?

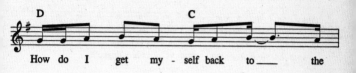

How do I get my-self back to ___ the

place where you said, ___ "I want some-thing ___

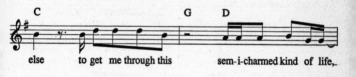

else to get me through this sem-i-charmed kind of life, ___

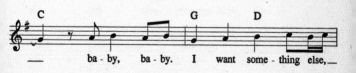

___ ba-by, ba-by. I want some-thing else, ___

D.S. al Coda I

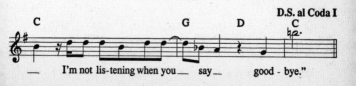

___ I'm not lis-tening when you ___ say ___ good-bye."

CODA I

plane came in,___ she said___ she was crash - ing.

The vel - vet, it rips in the cit - y. We tripped___

days you were wear - ing that vel - vet dress. ___

___ on the urge to feel ___ a - live, ___ but

You're the priest - ess, I must con - fess. Those

1.

now I'm strug - gling to sur - vive. ___ Those

2.

lit - tle red pant - ies, they pass the test. Slides

up a - round the bel - ly, face down on the mat - tress.

One, and you hold me, and we are bro - ken. ___ Still it's

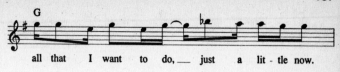

all that I want to do, __ just a lit - tle now.

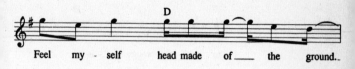

Feel my - self head made of __ the ground. __

__ I'm scared I'm not com - ing down. __ No, __ no, __

__ and I won't run for my __ life. __

She's got her jaws now locked down in a smile, __

__ but noth - ing is all __ right,

158

all right.___ I want___ some-thing else___

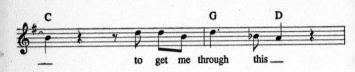

___ to get me through this ___

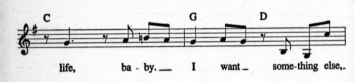

life, ba - by.___ I want___ some-thing else,___

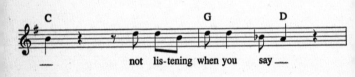

___ not lis-ten-ing when you say ___

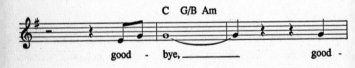

good - bye, _____ good -

bye, _____ good - bye, _____

D.C. al Coda II

good - bye.

CODA II

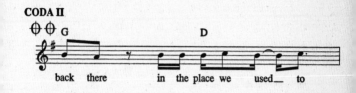

back there in the place we used to

start. Doo doo doot doo doo doot doo.

Doo doo doot doo doo doot doo.

Doo doo doot doo doo doot doo.

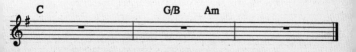

SHE DRIVES ME CRAZY

**Words and Music by DAVID STEELE
and ROLAND GIFT**

SIMPLY IRRESISTIBLE

**Words and Music by
ROBERT PALMER**

Hard Rock beat

How can it be per-mis-si-ble?
lov-ing is so pow-er-ful,
meth-ods are in-scru-ta-ble!

She com-pro-mise my prin-ci-ple.
it's sim-ply un-a-void-a-ble.
The proof is ir-re-fu-ta-ble.

Yeah, yeah.
Whoa, whoa. —
That
The
She's

kind of love is myth-i-cal;
trend is ir-re-vers-i-ble,
so com-plete-ly kiss-a-ble,

she's an — y-thing but typ-i-cal. —
the wom — an is in-vin-ci-ble. —
our lives — are in-di-vis-i-ble.

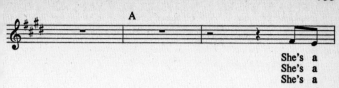

A

She's a
She's a
She's a

B5

craze you'd en-dorse; she's a pow-er-ful force._ You're o-
nat-u-ral law_ and she leaves me in awe._ She de-
craze you'd en-dorse; she's a pow-er-ful force._ You're o-

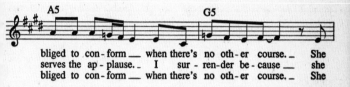

A5   **G5**

bliged to con-form_ when there's no oth-er course._ She
serves the ap-plause. I sur-ren-der be-cause_ she
bliged to con-form_ when there's no oth-er course._ She

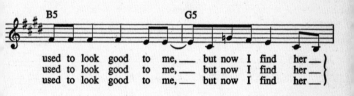

B5   **G5**

used to look good to me,_ but now I find her_)
used to look good to me,_ but now I find her_ }
used to look good to me,_ but now I find her_)

N.C.

sim-ply ir-re-

E5   **A**

sist-i-ble,

sim-ply ir - re - sist - i - ble.

Her

She's so fine, there's no tell-ing where the mon-ey went.

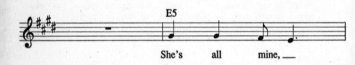

She's all mine, ___

To Coda ⊕

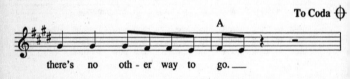

there's no oth-er way to go. ___

She's un - a - void - a - ble; I'm

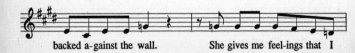

backed a-gainst the wall. She gives me feel-ings that I

SOME LIKE IT HOT

**Words and Music by ROBERT PALMER,
ANDY TAYLOR and JOHN TAYLOR**

Driving Dance beat

Em7

We want to mul - ti - ply; _____
at your side; _____

(D.S.) *Guitar solo*

_____ are you gon - na do ____ it?
_____ are you gon - na do ____ it?

I know you qua - li - fy;
She wants to be your ____ bride;

_____ are you gon - na do ____ it?
_____ are you gon - na do ____ it?

Don't be so cir - cum - scribe; _____
She wants to mul - ti - ply; _____

_____ are you gon - na do ____ it?
_____ are you gon - na do ____ it?

Just get your - self un - tied; _____
I know you won't be sat - is - fied _____

___ are you gon - na do __ it? ⎱
___ un - til you do __ it? ⎰

Solo ends   Feel   the heat _____

D/C Dsus/C   D   Dsus

Em

push - ing   you   to   de - cide. _____

D/C   Dsus/C   D   Dsus

Feel   the   heat _____

Em

burn - ing   you   up,   rea - dy   or   not.

Some   like __ it   hot,   and __ some

sweat when __ the heat is on. ____

Some feel __ the heat and __ de -

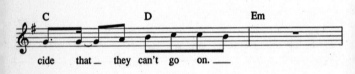

cide that __ they can't go on. ___

Some like __ it hot, but __ you

can't tell __ how hot till __ you try. ___

Some like __ it hot, so __ let's

turn up ___ the heat till ___ we

fry. ___

The girl is

(Instrumental)

CODA

fry. ___

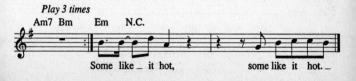

Some like _ it hot,   some like it hot. _

Some like _ it hot,   some like it hot. _

SWEET DREAMS
(Are Made of This)

Words and Music by
DAVID A. STEWART and ANNIE LENNOX

Moderately

(1.,2.) Sweet dreams are made of this.
(D.C.) *Instrumental solo*

Who am I to dis - a - gree? I

trav - el the world and the sev - en seas;

ev - 'ry - bod - y's look - ing for some - thing.
Solo ends

Some of them want to use you,

some of them want to get used by you.

Some of them want to a-buse __ you,

some of them want to be __ a-bused. __

(Instrumental)

Hold your head up, keep your head up, mov-in' on. __

Hold your head up, mov-in' on. __ Keep your head up, mov-in' on. __

Hold your head up, mov-in' on. __ Keep your head up, mov-in' on. __

D.C. and Fade (with repeats)

Hold your head up, mov-in' on. __ Keep your head up.

SWEET SURRENDER

Words and Music by
SARAH McLACHLAN

175

TEARS IN HEAVEN

Words and Music by ERIC CLAPTON
and WILL JENNINGS

Would you know my name
Would you hold my hand
Would you know my name

if I saw you in heav - en?
if I saw you in heav - en?
if I saw you in heav - en?

Would it be the same
Would you help me stand
Would you be the same

if I saw you in heav - en?
if I saw you in heav - en?
if I saw you in heav - en?

(1.,3.) I must be strong
(2.) I'll find my way

and car - ry on ____ 'cause I know_
through night and day ____ 'cause I know_

I don't be - long ____ here in heav -
I just can't stay ____ here in heav -

To Coda

en.
en.

Time can bring you down,_
_ time can bend your knees. _

Time can break the heart, ____ have you beg - gin' please,_
_ beg - gin' please. ____

Be-yond the door __

there's peace, I'm sure. __ And I know

__ there'll be no more __ tears in heav-

D.C. al Coda

en.

CODA

en.

TOTAL ECLIPSE OF
THE HEART

Words and Music by
JIM STEINMAN

Rock Ballad

(Turn a - round) _ Ev - 'ry now and then I get a
part.
(Turn a - round) _ Ev - 'ry now and then I get a
Instrumental solo

lit - tle bit lone - ly and you're nev - er com - ing 'round.
lit - tle bit rest - less and I dream of some-thing wild. _

(Turn a - round) _ Ev - 'ry now and then I get a
(Turn a - round) _ Ev - 'ry now and then I get a

lit - tle bit tired ____ of lis - t'ning to the sound of my tears.
lit - tle bit help - less and I'm ly - ing like a child in your arms.

(Turn a - round) _ Ev - 'ry now and then I get a
(Turn a - round) _ Ev - 'ry now and then I get a

lit - tle bit ner - vous that the best of all the years have gone by.
lit - tle bit an - gry and I know I've got to get out and cry.

Db

(Turn a - round) _ Ev - 'ry now and then I get a
(Turn a - round) _ Ev - 'ry now and then I get a

B

lit - tle bit ter - ri-fied and then I see the look in your eyes.)
lit - tle bit ter - ri-fied but then I see the look in your eyes.
Solo ends)

E   **E/A** **A**

(Turn a - round _ bright _ eyes) Ev - 'ry now and then I fall a -

1
E   **E/A** **A**

part. ____ Ev - 'ry now and then I fall a -
(Turn a - round _ bright _ eyes)

2, 3
E   **E/A** **A**

part. ____ Ev - 'ry now and then I fall a -
(Turn a - round _ bright _ eyes) _

Ab   **Fm**

part,   and I need you now _ to - night,

Db   **Eb7**

and I need you more _ than ev -

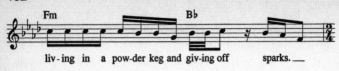

Fm   **Bb**

liv-ing in a pow-der keg and giv-ing off   sparks. ___

I real-ly need you to-night.

Ab/C   **Eb/Bb**   **Ab/C**

For-ev - er's gon-na start to-night, ___

Db   **Eb7**

___ for-ev - er's gon-na start ___ to -

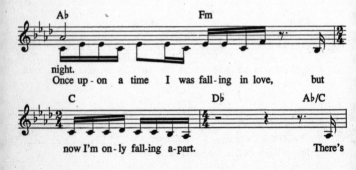

Ab   **Fm**

night.
Once up-on a time I was fall-ing in love,   but

C   **Db**   **Ab/C**

now I'm on-ly fall-ing a-part.   There's

Bbm7   **Eb7b9**

noth-ing I can do; a to-tal e-clipse ___ of the heart. __

(Instrumental)

Once up-on a time there was light in my life, but

now there's on - ly love in the dark.

Nothing I can say; a to-tal e-clipse of the heart.

(Instrumental)

D.C. al Coda

CODA

Nothing I can say; a to-tal e-clipse of the heart,

Repeat ad lib. and Fade

a to-tal e-clipse of the heart.

COUNTING BLUE CARS

Words by J.R. RICHARDS
Music by SCOT ALEXANDER, GEORGE PENDERGAST,
RODNEY BROWNING, J.R. RICHARDS and GREGORY KOLANEK

Moderate Rock

your thoughts on God, — 'cause I'd

real - ly like — to meet — her. _____

And ask her why — we're who — we are. —

Tell me all —

your thoughts — on God, — 'cause I'm on —

my way — to see — her. _____

So tell me, am___ I ver - y

far, _____ am I ver - y far_

___ now?"___ *(Instrumental)*

D.C. al Coda

CODA

Tell me all _

___ your thoughts_ on God, ___

{ 'cause I'd
{ 'cause I'm

real - ly like __ to meet __ her. _____
on my way __ to see __ her. _____

D   1
         E7

And ask her why __ we're who __ we are. _
So tell me, am __

G

2 E7   G

__ I ver - y   far, _____

                    D

__ am I ver - y far __ now? Tell me all __

E7   G

__ your thoughts __ on God. __

            1,2   3
            D   Bm

            Tell me   all __

IT'S STILL ROCK AND ROLL TO ME

Words and Music by
BILLY JOEL

Moderately fast Rock/Shuffle

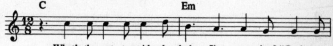

What's the mat - ter with the clothes I'm wear - ing? "Can't you
What's the mat - ter with the car I'm driv - ing? "Can't you
How a - bout a pair of pink side wind - ers and a
What's the mat - ter with the crowd I'm see - ing? "Don't you

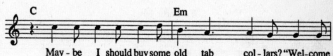

tell that your tie's too wide?" __
tell that it's out of style?" __
bright or - ange pair of pants? __
know that they're out of touch?" __

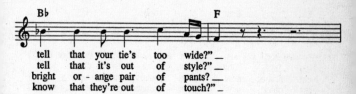

May - be I should buy some old tab col - lars? "Wel - come
Should I get a set of white wall tires? __ "Are you
"Well you could real - ly be a Beau Brum - mel, ba - by, if you
Should I try to be a straight 'A' stu - dent? "If you

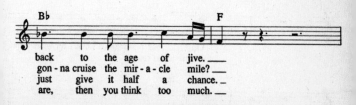

back to the age of jive. __
gon - na cruise the mir - a - cle mile? __
just give it half a chance. __
are, then you think too much. __

190

Where have you been hid-in' out late-ly, hon-ey? You
Now-a-days you can't be too sen-ti-men-tal. Your
Don't waste your mon-ey on a new set of speak-ers. You
Don't you know a-bout the new fash-ion, hon-ey?

can't dress trash-y till you spend a lot of mon-ey."
best bet's a true ba-by blue Con - ti-nen-tal."
get more mile-age from a cheap pair of sneak-ers."
All you need are looks and a whole lot of mon-ey." It's the

Ev-'ry-bod-y's talk-in' 'bout the new sound. Fun-ny, but
Hot funk, cool punk, e-ven if it's old junk,
Next phase, new wave, dance craze, an-y-ways
next phase, new wave, dance craze, an-y-ways

it's

To Coda

still rock and roll to me.

Oh, _____ it does-n't mat-ter what they
Instrumental solo

say in the pa-pers 'cause it's al-ways been the same old _ scene. _

TWO PRINCES

Words and Music by
SPIN DOCTORS

Moderately fast

(1.,4.) One, two   princ-es kneel be-fore you. (That's what I said,_ now.)
(2.) This one,   he got a prince-ly rack-et. (That's what I said,_ now.)
(3.) *Instrumental solo*

Princ-es,   princ-es who _ a-dore _ you. (Just go a-head,_ now.)
Got some   big seal up-on _ his jack-et, (ain't in his head,_ now.)

One has   dia-monds in _ his pock-ets, (that's some bread,_ now.)
Mar-ry him, your fa-ther will con-done you. (How 'bout that,_ now.) You

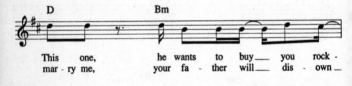

This   one,   he wants to buy_ you rock-
mar-ry me,   your fa-ther will_ dis-own_

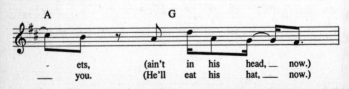

_ ets,   (ain't in his head, _ now.)
_ you.   (He'll eat his hat, _ now.)

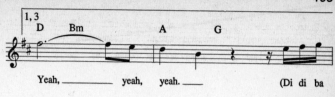

1, 3

D   Bm   A   G

Yeah, _____ yeah, yeah. ___   (Di di ba

D   Bm

dip.   Di dip   dip   di dip.   Ba dee-dle-ee

A   G

di ba du ba du ba du ba du ba du ba du ba du ba.)

Solo ends

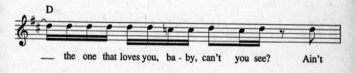

2,4

G7

Mar - ry   him   or   mar - ry   me.   I'm _

D

_ the one that loves you, ba - by, can't you see?   Ain't

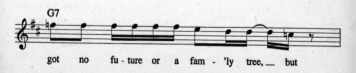

G7

got   no   fu - ture or a fam - 'ly tree, _ but

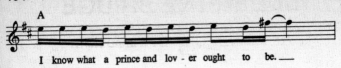

I know what a prince and lov - er ought to be. ___

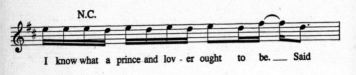

N.C.

I know what a prince and lov - er ought to be. ___ Said

D Bm A G

if you want to call_ me, ba - by, (just go a - head,_ now.) And

D Bm A G

if you want to tell_ me may - be, (just go a - head,_ now.) And

D Bm A G

if you wan-na buy_ me flow - ers, (just go a - head,_ now.) And

D.C. and Fade
after 4th ending

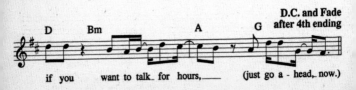

D Bm A G

if you want to talk_ for hours,___ (just go a - head,_ now.)

UNDER THE BRIDGE

**Words and Music by ANTHONY KIEDIS,
FLEA, JOHN FRUSCIANTE and CHAD SMITH**

Slow Rock Ballad

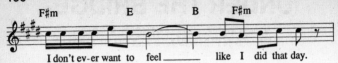

I don't ev-er want to feel ____ like I did that day.

Take me to the place I love, ____ take me all the way.__

I don't ev-er want to feel ____ like I did that day.

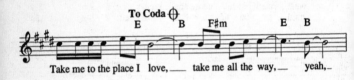

To Coda

Take me to the place I love, ___ take me all the way, ___ yeah,__

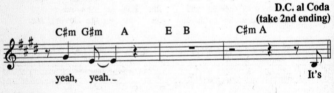

D.C. al Coda
(take 2nd ending)

yeah, yeah.__ It's

CODA

___ take me all the way, _____ yeah, _

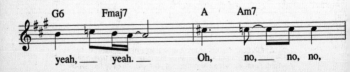

yeah, ___ yeah. ___ Oh, no, no, no,

yeah, ___ yeah. ___ Love me, ___ I said,

yeah, ___ yeah. ___ One time.

Un-der the bridge ___ down-town is where I drew some blood.

Un-der the bridge ___ down-town I could not get e - nough. __

Un-der the bridge ___ down-town, for - got a - bout my love.

Un-der the bridge ___ down-town I gave my life a - way. ___

Play 8 times

___ Vocal ad lib.

UP WHERE WE BELONG

from the Paramount Picture
AN OFFICER AND A GENTLEMAN

Words by WILL JENNINGS
Music by BUFFY SAINTE-MARIE and JACK NITZSCHE

no   time   to   cry, _____

life's   you   and   I, _____   a -

live, _____   to - day. _____

Love lift us up where we be-long, _ where the

ea - gles cry _ on a moun - tain high. _

Love lift us up where we be-long, _ far from the

Repeat ad lib. and Fade

world we know, _ where the clear winds blow. _

VISION OF LOVE

**Words and Music by MARIAH CAREY
and BEN MARGULIES**

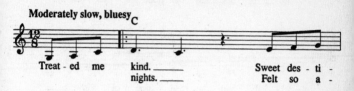

Treat - ed me kind. _____ Sweet des - ti -
nights. _____ Felt so a -

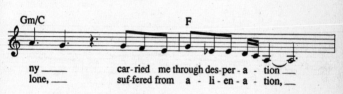

ny _____ car - ried me through des - per - a - tion _____
lone, _____ suf - fered from a - li - en - a - tion,

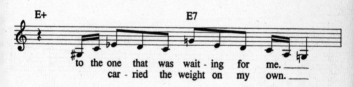

to the one that was wait - ing for me.
car - ried the weight on my own. _____

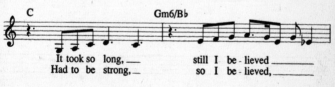

It took so long, _____ still I be - lieved _____
Had to be strong, _____ so I be - lieved,

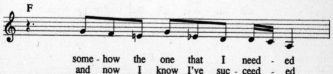

some - how the one that I need - ed
and now I know I've suc - ceed - ed

202

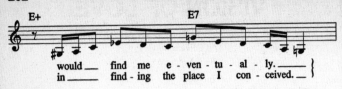

would ___ find me e - ven - tu - al - ly. ___ }
in ___ find - ing the place I con - ceived. ___

I had a vi - sion of love ___

and it was all that you've giv - en to

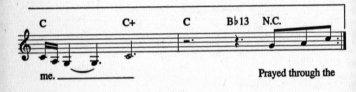

me. ___ Prayed through the

and it was all that you've giv - en to

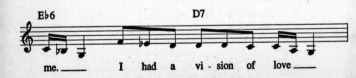

me. ___ I had a vi - sion of love ___

WALKING ON BROKEN GLASS

Words and Music by
ANNIE LENNOX

WE DIDN'T START THE FIRE

Words and Music by
BILLY JOEL

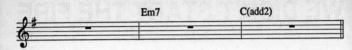

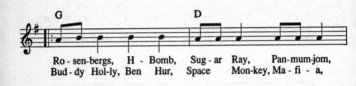

Ro - sen-bergs,　H - Bomb,　Sug - ar Ray,　Pan-mum-jom,
Bud - dy Hol-ly,　Ben Hur,　Space　Mon-key, Ma - fi - a,

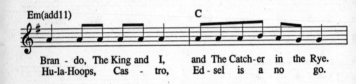

Bran - do, The King and　I,　and The Catch-er　in　the Rye.
Hu-la-Hoops,　Cas - tro,　Ed - sel　is　a　no　go.

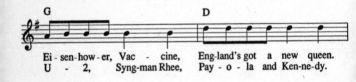

Ei - sen-how - er, Vac - cine,　Eng-land's got　a　new queen.
U - 2,　Syng-man Rhee,　Pay - o - la and Ken-ne-dy.

Mar - ci - an - o,　Li - ber - a - ce,
Chub - by Check - er,　Psy - cho,

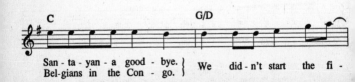

San - ta - yan - a good - bye. }　We　did - n't start　the fi -
Bel-gians in the Con - go. }

Em7

-re.   It was al-ways burn-ing since the

C(add2)   **G/D**

world's been turn-ing.   We did-n't start the fi-

G/B

-re.   No, we did-n't light it, but we

C(add2)   𝄋 **G**

tried to fight it.   { Jo-seph Sta-lin, Ma-len-kov,
Hem-ing-way, Eich-mann,
(D.S.) Birth Con-trol, Ho Chi Minh,

D   **Em(add11)**

Nas-ser and Pro-ko-fi-ev, Rock-e-fel-ler, Cam-pa-nel-la,
Strang-er in a Strange Land. Dy-lan, Ber-lin,
Rich-ard Nix-on back a-gain. Moon-shot, Wood-stock,

C   **G**

Com-mu-nist Bloc. Roy Cohn, Juan Pe-rón,
Bay of Pigs In-va-sion. Law-rence of A-ra-bi-a,
Wa-ter-gate, Punk Rock, Be-gin, Rea-gan, Pal-es-tine,

D   **Em(add11)**

Tos-ca-ni-ni, Da-cron. Dien Bien Phu Falls,
Brit-ish Bea-tle-ma-ni-a. Ole Miss, John Glenn,
Ter-ror on the air-line. Ay-ah-toll-ahs in I-ran,

G/D
We did-n't start the fi - re. No, we

G/B ... **Am7**
did - n't light _ it, but we tried to fight _ it.

C ... **Am**
Lit - tle Rock, Pas - ter - nak, Mic - key Man - tle, Ker - ou - ac,

Em ... **D**
Sput - nik, Chou En - Lai, Bridge on the Riv - er Kwai,

C ... **Am**
Leb - a - non, Charles de Gaulle, Cal - i - for - nia base - ball,

Em ... **D**
Stark - weath - er Hom - i - cide, Chil - dren of Tha - lid - o - mide.

Oh, _____

2

C   G/D

what else do I have to say? We did-n't start the fi-

Em7

- re.   It was al - ways burn - ing since the

C(add2)   G/D

world's been turn - ing.   We did-n't start the fi-

G/B

- re.   No, we did - n't light _ it, but we

C(add2)   D.S. al Coda   CODA

C

tried to fight _ it.   AIDS, Crack, Ber-nie Goetz.

G   D

Hy - po - der-mics on the shores, Chi-na's un - der mar-tial law.

Em   N.C.

Rock and Roll - er Co - la Wars, I can't take it an - y-more.

WE GOT THE BEAT

Words and Music by
CHARLOTTE CAFFEY

Moderately fast Rock

See the peo - ple walk-ing down the street;
See the kids just get - ting out of school.
Go - Go mu - sic real - ly makes us dance.

fall in line just watch - ing all their feet. ___
They can't wait to hang ___ out and be cool. ___
Do the po - ny; puts ___ us in a trance. ___

They don't know where ___ they want to go, but they're
Hang a - round 'til quar - ter af - ter twelve; that's
Do the wa - tu - si, just ___ give us a chance; that's

walk - ing in time.
when they fall in line.
when we fall in line.

(1., 2.) They got the beat, ___
(3.) We got the beat, ___

___ they got the ___ beat, {they} {kids} got the ___
___ we got the ___ beat, we got the ___

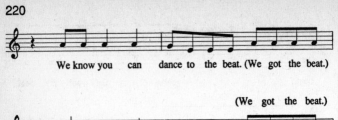

We know you can dance to the beat. (We got the beat.)

(We got the beat.)

Jump back, ___ get down.

E

'Round and 'round and 'round.

A5

(We got the beat.) We got the beat.

(We got the beat.) We got the beat.

(We got the beat. We got the beat.) We got the beat.

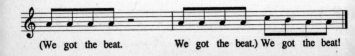

(We got the beat. We got the beat.) We got the beat!

WITH EVERY BEAT OF MY HEART

Words and Music by TOMMY FARAGHER, LOTTI GOLDEN and ARTHUR BAKER

With energy

Who, __ uh. Ah - ah - ah - ah.

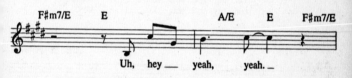

Uh, hey __ yeah, yeah. __

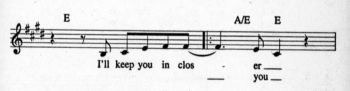

I'll keep you in clos - er __
__ you __

to the love I know.
more ev - er - y day.

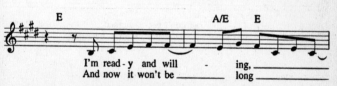

I'm read - y and will - ing, _____
And now it won't be _____ long _____

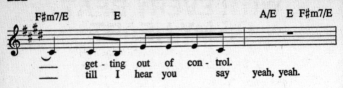

— get - ting out of con - trol.
— till I hear you say yeah, yeah.

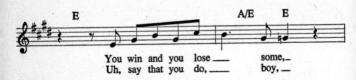

You win and you lose ___ some, ___
Uh, say that you do, ___ boy, ___

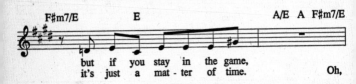

but if you stay in the game,
it's just a mat - ter of time. Oh,

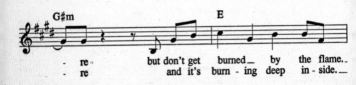

be - fore you know it, (1., D.S.) you'll feel the fi -
be - fore you know it, (2.) you'll feel the fi -

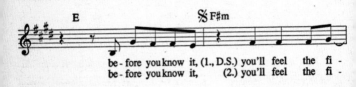

- re but don't get burned ___ by the flame..
- re and it's burn - ing deep in - side. ___

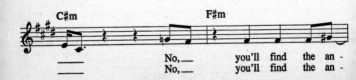

___ No, ___ you'll find the an -
___ No, ___ you'll find the an -

224

WHAT'S UP

Words and Music by
LINDA PERRY

Twen-ty-five years of my life, and still __ I'm
And I try, oh my God, do I

trying to get up that great big hill __ of hope
try, I try all the time

for a des-ti - na - tion.
in this in-sti - tu - tion.

I
And

real-ize quick - ly when I know I should, _ that the world _
I pray, oh my God, __ do I pray, _

Bm ... **D**

_ was made up of this broth-er - hood _ of man,
— I pray ev - 'ry sin-gle day

A

for what-ev - er that means. _ }
for a rev-o - lu - tion. __ }

And so I

cry some - times when I'm ly - in' in bed __ just to

Bm

get it all out, _ what's in _____ my head, _ and I,

D ... **A**

I am feel-ing a lit-tle pe-cu - liar.

And so I wake in the morn-ing and I

228

WHERE HAVE ALL
THE COWBOYS GONE?

Words and Music by
PAULA COLE

Moderately fast Rock

Doo dit, doo doo dit, doo doo dit, doo doo dit, doo

doo dit, doo doo dit, doo doo dit, doo doo dit, doo

doo dit, doo doo dit, doo doo dit, doo doo dit, doo

doo dit, doo doo dit, doo doo dit, doo doo.

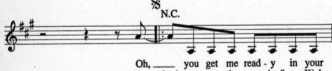

Oh, ____ you get me read-y in your
don't you stay the eve-ning? Kick
fi - n'lly sold the Chev-y when we

fif - ty - six Chev-y. Why don't we go sit down in the shade?
back and watch the T V, and I'll fix a lit - tle some-thing to eat.
had an - oth-er ba - by and you took that job in Ten - nes-see.

233

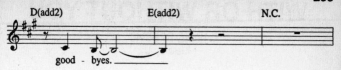

good - byes. _____

D.S. al Coda

CODA

E(add2)

Spoken: We

- boys gone? ___

F#m   C#m

Where is my Marl-bor-o Man? _

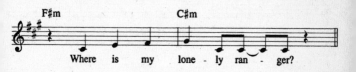

F#m   C#m

Where is his shin-y gun? _____

F#m   C#m

Where is my lone-ly ran-ger?

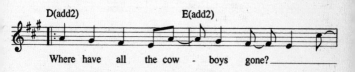

D(add2)   E(add2)

Where have all the cow-boys gone? _____

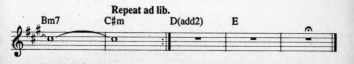

Repeat ad lib.

Bm7   C#m   D(add2)   E

WITH OR WITHOUT YOU

Words by BONO
Music by U2

Moderately

See the stone ___ set in your eyes.

___ See the thorn ___ twist in your side. ___

___ I'll wait ___ for you.

Sleight of hand ___ and twist of fate, ___
Through the storm ___ we reach the shore. ___

___ on a bed of nails ___ she makes me wait.
You give it all ___ but I want more.

And I wait ___ with-out ___ you.
And I'm wait ___ ing for ___ you.

Bb7sus   Cm7

with or with - out you, ___ uh - huh. ___

Ab   Eb   Bb7sus

___ I can't live ___ with or with-

Cm   Ab   Eb

out ___ you, with or with - out you. ___

(Instrumental)

Ah, ___ ah, ___

Eb

___ *(Instrumental)*

Repeat and Fade

Bbsus   Cm   Ab5

ZOMBIE

Lyrics and Music by
DOLORES O'RIORDAN

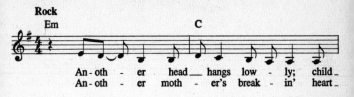

An - oth - er head ___ hangs low - ly; child ___
An - oth - er moth - er's break - in' heart ___

___ is slow - ly tak - en.
___ is tak - ing o - ver.

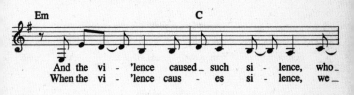

And the vi - 'lence caused ___ such si - lence, who ___
When the vi - 'lence caus - es si - lence, we ___

___ are we mis - tak - en? But you see,
___ must be mis - tak - en. It's the same

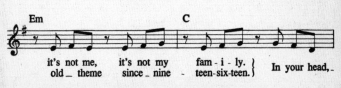

it's not me, it's not my fam - i - ly. } In your head, ___
old ___ theme since ___ nine - teen - six - teen.

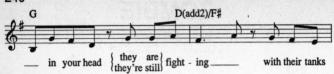

_ in your head { they are / they're still } fight - ing ____ with their tanks

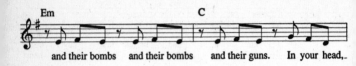

and their bombs   and their bombs   and their guns.   In your head,_

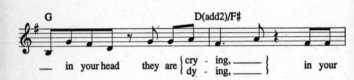

_ in your head   they are { cry - ing, ____ / dy - ing, ____ }   in your

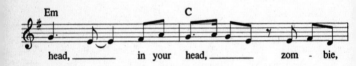

head, ____   in your   head, ____   zom - bie,

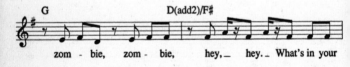

zom - bie,   zom - bie,   hey,_   hey._   What's in your

head, ____   in your   head, ____   zom - bie,

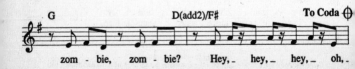

zom - bie,   zom - bie?   Hey,_   hey,_   hey,_   oh,_

241

WONDERWALL

Words and Music by
NOEL GALLAGHER

Moderately

To - day is gon - na be the day that they're

gon - na throw it back to you. __

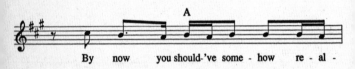

By now you should-'ve some - how re - al -

ized what you got - ta do. __

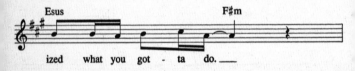

I don't be - lieve __ that an - y - bod - y

feels the way I do __ a-bout you now. ____

Back-beat the word was on the street that the
To-day was gon-na be the day, but they'll

fi-re in your heart is out. __
nev-er throw it back to you. __

I'm sure you've heard it all be-fore but you
By now you should-'ve some-how re-al-

nev-er real-ly had a doubt. __ }
ized what you're not to do. __ }

I don't be-lieve __ that an - y - bo - dy

feels the way I do __ a-bout you now..

__ { And all __
{ And all __

244

YOU GIVE LOVE A BAD NAME

Words and Music by JON BON JOVI,
RICHIE SAMBORA and DESMOND CHILD

Moderate Rock

(Instrumental)

An an-gel's smile __ is what you sell. You
You paint your smile __ on your lips,

prom-ise me heav-en then put me through hell. __
blood-red nails on your fin - ger-tips. __ A

Chains of __ love got a hold on me. When
school-boy's dream, you act so shy. Your

pas-sion's a pris-on, you can't break __ free.
ver-y first kiss was your first kiss good-bye.

Whoa, __ you're a load-ed gun. __ Yeah. __

YOU LEARN

Lyrics by ALANIS MORISSETTE
Music by ALANIS MORISSETTE and GLEN BALLARD

MCA Music Publishing

Swal - low _____ it down. __
Throw _____ it down. __
Wear _____ it out, __

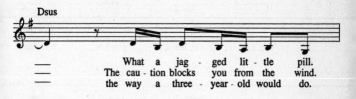

__ What a jag - ged lit - tle pill.
__ The cau - tion blocks you from the wind.
__ the way a three - year - old would do.

It feels _____ so good __
Hold _____ it up __
Melt _____ it down. __

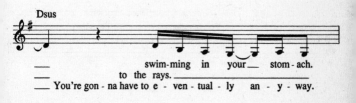

__ swim - ming in your __ stom - ach.
__ to the rays. _____
__ You're gon - na have to e - ven - tual - ly an - y - way.

Wait un - til _____ the
You wait _____ and _____
The fire _____ trucks __

GUITAR CHORD FRAMES

	C	Cm	C+	C6	Cm6
C					

	C#	C#m	C#+	C#6	C#m6
C#/Db					

	D	Dm	D+	D6	Dm6
D					

	Eb	Ebm	Eb+	Eb6	Ebm6
Eb/D#					

	E	Em	E+	E6	Em6
E					

	F	Fm	F+	F6	Fm6
F					

This guitar chord reference includes 120 commonly used chords. For a more complete guide to guitar chords, see "THE PAPERBACK CHORD BOOK" (HL00702009).

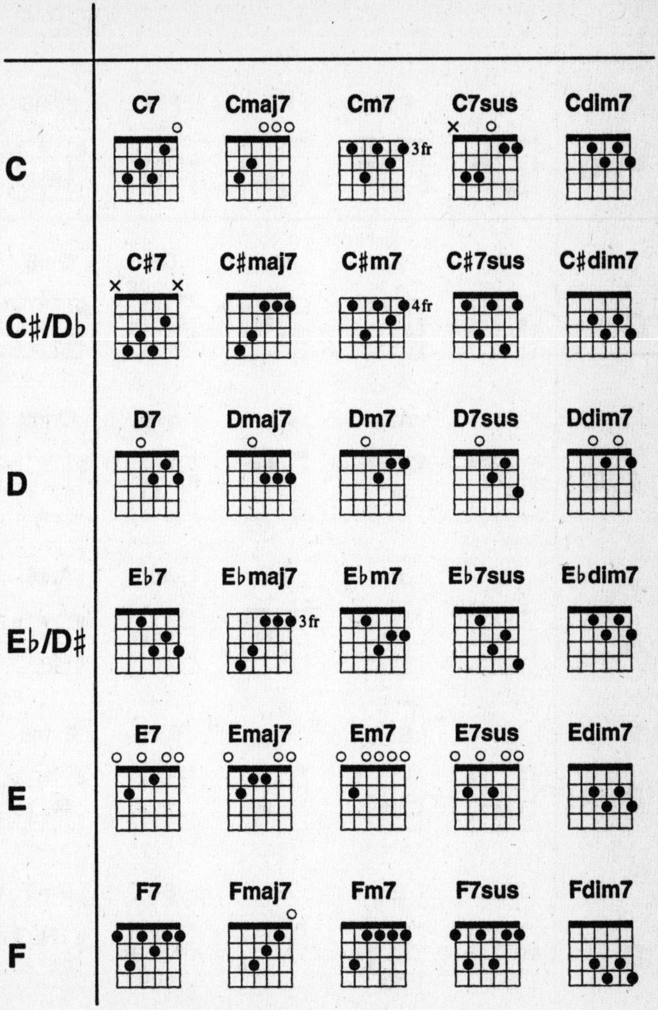
C
C7
Cmaj7
Cm7
3fr
C7sus
Cdim7
C♯/D♭
C♯7
C♯maj7
C♯m7
4fr
C♯7sus
C♯dim7
D
D7
Dmaj7
Dm7
D7sus
Ddim7
E♭/D♯
E♭7
E♭maj7
3fr
E♭m7
E♭7sus
E♭dim7
E
E7
Emaj7
Em7
E7sus
Edim7
F
F7
Fmaj7
Fm7
F7sus
Fdim7

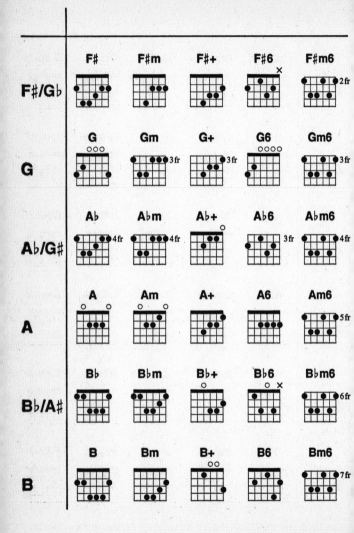

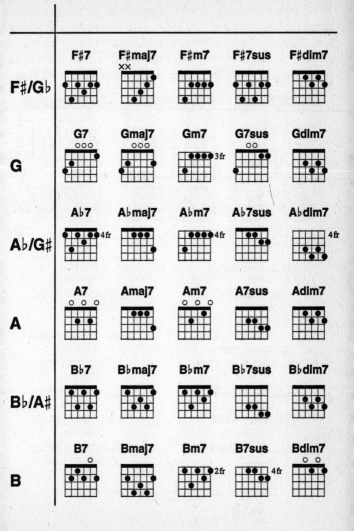

THE PAPERBACK SONGS SERIES

These perfectly portable paperbacks include the melodies, lyrics, and chords symbols for your favorite songs, all in a convenient, pocket-sized book. Using concise, one-line music notation, anyone from hobbyists to professionals can strum on the guitar, play melodies on the piano, or sing the lyrics to great songs. Books also include a helpful guitar chord chart.

'80s & '90s ROCK
00240126

THE BEATLES
00702008

THE BLUES
00702014

**CHORDS FOR
KEYBOARD & GUITAR**
00702009

CLASSIC ROCK
00310058

COUNTRY HITS
00702013

NEIL DIAMOND
00702012

HYMNS
00240103

**INTERNATIONAL
FOLKSONGS**
00240104

JAZZ STANDARDS
00240114

MOTOWN HITS
00240125

MOVIE MUSIC
00240113

ELVIS PRESLEY
00240102

**THE ROCK & ROLL
COLLECTION**
00702020

FOR MORE INFORMATION, SEE YOUR LOCAL MUSIC DEALER,
OR WRITE TO:

HAL•LEONARD®
CORPORATION
7777 W. BLUEMOUND RD. P.O. BOX 13819 MILWAUKEE, WI 53213